C000110200

1 MONTH OF
FREE
READING

at
www.ForgottenBooks.com

By purchasing this book you are eligible for one month membership to ForgottenBooks.com, giving you unlimited access to our entire collection of over 1,000,000 titles via our web site and mobile apps.

To claim your free month visit: www.forgottenbooks.com/free1118156

ISBN 978-0-331-39814-4
PIBN 11118156

Historic, Archive Document

Do not assume content reflects current scientific knowledge, policies, or practices.

MAY 1947

MARKETING ACTIVITIES

/⁰/₅

U. S. Department of Agriculture
Production and Marketing Administration
Washington 25, D.C.

IN THIS ISSUE:

Address all inquiries to
The Editor, Marketing Activities
Production and Marketing Admin.
U. S. Department of Agriculture
Washington 25, D. C.

Issued monthly. Vol. 10, No. 5

Iceless Refrigerator Car
Car Tested by USDA

....By H. D. Johnson and D. H. Rose

Frozen foods must be stored and transported at near-zero tempera_
tures if they are to retain their prime quality. Tests recently conclud_
ed by the U.S. Department of Agriculture indicate that a newly developed
refrigerator car is able to maintain a commodity temperature of approxi_
mately 0°F., even under conditions of summer heat. The ordinary refrigerator car, which uses ice and salt is unable to hold a temperature much
below 15°F. Fan cars and overhead bunker cars can maintain temperatures
substantially lower than 15°F., but not as low as 0°F.

The refrigeration system used in the experimental car is a new ap-
plication of an old principle. The refrigerant--liquid anhydrous ammonia
--is contained in receiving tanks with a capacity of 1,900 pounds. The
flow of ammonia to the expansion (cooling) coils located in the ceiling
of the car is controlled by a bulb-type temperature-control apparatus
with a range of from -5°F. to 65°F. After passing through a surge tank
and expanding at low pressure in the cooling coils, the ammonia passes
into absorber tanks where it is taken up by water. These tanks have a
capacity of approximately 750 gallons of water. The tanks are usually
charged with only 500 gallons, however, to allow for expansion as the
ammonia enters. Both the ammonia and water tanks are suspended under the
car with a clearance well within the limits established by the Association of American Railroads. The refrigeration system has no moving parts
and hence no power requirements. (See illustration).

The car itself has a total loading capacity of 1,938 cubic feet.
Insulation specifications for side and end walls call for two 1½ inch
layers of Naturezone, with a 2-inch air space between the layers; two
layers of Silvercote over the outside layer of Naturezone, and one layer
inside the inside layer of Naturezone. The floor is covered with 2 inches of Naturezone with ½ inch of Celotex; the roof with 4½ inches of
Haircraft. The car was built by the North American Car Corporation.

To determine the efficiency of the car in actual operation, the
Frigid Transport Corporation, patentees of the refrigeration system and
the Birds Eye-Snyder Division of General Foods Corporation requested the
U. S. Department of Agriculture to conduct tests.

On February 10, 1947, the car was loaded at Jersey City, N.J., with
frozen tangerine segments furnished by the Birds Eye-Snyder Division.
The car moved from Jersey City to Alexandria, Va., where it was put in a
test house owned by the Fruit Growers Express Company. To simulate hot
weather conditions, the air in the test house and surrounding the refrigerator car was maintained continuously at around 92°F. with special
equipment. The car was returned to Jersey City on February 24.

Thermometers were placed in various positions throughout the car at
the time of loading and additional thermometers were installed during

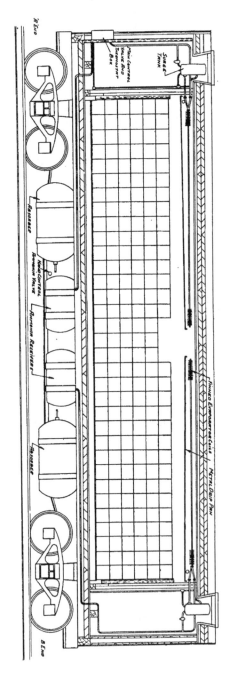

In the experimental car the refrigerant used is liquid anhydrous ammonia. This is c ntained in receiving tanks having a capacity of 1,900 pounds. The flow of ammonia to the expansion (cooling) coils located in the ceiling of the car is controlled by a bulb-type temperature-control apparatus with a range of from -5° F. to 65° F. After passing through the surge tank and expanding at low pressure in the cooling coils, the ammonia passes int absorber tanks where it is taken up by water. These tanks have a capacity of approximately 750 gallons of water. The tanks are usually charged with only 500 gallons so as to allo w f r expansion as the ammonia enters. Both the ammonia and water tanks are suspended under the car with a clearance well within the limits established by the Association of American Railroads. The refrigeration system has no moving parts and no power requirements.

During the 10-day test conducted by the U. S. Department of Agriculture, the ammonia-consumption rate averaged 41.98 pounds per hour, and 46 hours elapsed between rechargings during one period. With proper "service stations," the ammonia absorbed by the water may be recovered by distillation and used again.

the period the car was in the test house. Temperature readings were taken at Jersey City, Baltimore, and upon arrival at Alexandria. Thereafter readings of temperature of air and commodity inside the car, and air outside the car in the test house, were made at intervals of 2 hours throughout the 10-day period the test was conducted.

The results of the car testing experiment showed that, under conditions of this test, the average top commodity temperatures ranged from about 4°F. to nearly 1°F; the bottom commodity temperatures ranged from about -3°F. to about 3°F. (Improved wall and floor racks, allowing a freer circulation of air, would undoubtedly narrow the spread between temperatures at the top of the load and those at the bottom of the load.) The tangerine segments were frozen when they were loaded in the car; they were still hard frozen when they were unloaded.

From the time the test started on February 10 until it ended on February 21, the ammonia-consumption rate was 41.98 pounds per hour. During one 46-hour period that elapsed between rechargings the rate was 45.45 pounds per hour.

Inasmuch as the test house was not equipped to handle water under pressure or liquid ammonia, the improvised method of charging took longer than would be required at a "service station" equipped for that purpose. It should also be mentioned that when the absorption tanks were drained, the ammonia-charged water was discarded, whereas, with proper equipment, the ammonia could be recovered by distillation and used again.

(A detailed description of this test is presented in "Test of Refrigerator Car Equipped with Split-Absorption System of Refrigeration," a report by H. D. Johnson and D. H. Rose. Copies may be obtained upon request to Information Service, Production and Marketing Administration, U. S. Department of Agriculture, Washington 25, D. C.

Names of commercial firms and products are mentioned in this article. This does not imply endorsement of the firms or products by the U. S. Department of Agriculture.--Editor's note.)

PLENTIFUL FOODS FOR JUNE

A number of canned foods are included on the list of plentiful foods for June--peas (standard grade), beets, carrots, tomato juice, sauerkraut, citrus juice, and grapefruit segments. Also listed are potatoes, oranges and grapefruit, bulk sauerkraut, peanut butter, and cottage cheese. Large stocks of dried peaches and prunes are available, especially in the smaller sizes and are expected to be offered at somewhat lower retail prices. Frozen vegetables, particularly frozen peas and spinach, are in good supply and have been materially reduced in some markets. Plentiful supplies of heavy tom turkeys will be available in many areas for hotels, restaurants, and other large users. (Note: The food items mentioned above are plentiful on a country-wide scale but may not be available in every locality.)

> This is another in a series of articles dealing with basic marketing programs of the U. S. Department of Agriculture. Previous discussions have covered price support and marketing agreement programs.—Editor

The Commodity Credit Corporation

... By Jesse B. Gilmer, President
Commodity Credit Corporation

The Commodity Credit Corporation, a Federal agency established by Congress,assists in stabilizing the production and marketing of American farm products. This the Corporation does through six general types of activity: (1) Price support programs, (2) supply programs, (3) foreign purchase programs, (4) commodity export programs, (5) subsidy programs, and (6) a loan to the Secretary of Agriculture for agricultural conservation purposes.

Organized under the laws of the State of Delaware in 1933, the Commodity Credit Corporation until late in 1939 was managed and operated in close affiliation with the Reconstruction Finance Corporation. In 1939, the Corporation was transferred to the U. S. Department of Agriculture and its operations placed under the supervision and control of the Secretary of Agriculture.

Program activities of the Corporation today are carried out through the facilities and personnel of the Department's Production and Marketing Administration. The various programs are formulated in their details by the appropriate branches of PMA. If approved by the Corporation, the programs are administered by units of PMA.

The board of directors of the Corporation includes the Secretary of Agriculture, who is the chairman;the Under Secretary of Agriculture; the Assistant Secretary of Agriculture; and six policy-making officials of PMA. The officers of the Corporation--president, vice presidents, treasurer,and secretary--are officials in policy-making positions in PMA.

In 1938, Congress authorized the Corporation to issue and have outstanding bonds, notes, debentures, and similar obligations in an amount not to exceed $500,000,000. The borrowing power of the Corporation has been increased by subsequent legislation, however, and today the Corporation is authorized to borrow $4,750,000,000 on the credit of the United States.

The scope of the Corporation's activities is indicated by the funds "applied" to the various programs. In 1945-46, for example, such funds totaled $3,538,000,000. Although these expenditures were offset to a large extent by sales of commodities acquired and other income,the Corporation—largely because of subsidy operations--ended up with a net loss of $830,000,000. During the current 1946-47 fiscal year, funds expended on the Corporation's programs are expected to total $2,530,000,000. With all subsidies discontinued during the year, except the one on sugar, the Corporation is expected to show a net gain of about $2,000,000 on its over-all operations.

The "life" of the Corporation generally has been measured in 2-year intervals. Thus Congressional action has been taken at least every two years authorizing the Corporation to continue as an agency of the Federal Government.

Price Support Programs

Price support activities of the Corporation have, as their name implies, the objective of establishing minimum prices to producers of certain farm commodities. Price support programs undoubtedly encouraged farmers to produce the large amounts of food and fiber needed during the war. And they have stimulated production needed to meet strong domestic and foreign demand for farm commodities during the present postwar readjustment period.

Because of the differences in price-support legislation passed by Congress at different times, price support programs are generally grouped into three general categories:

1. Prices of "basic" commodities—corn, wheat, rice, tobacco, and peanuts for nuts—are supported through mandatory loans at 90 percent of parity. The price of cotton, also a basic commodity, is supported by loans at 92½ percent of parity. These rates will be maintained through December 31, 1948.

After that date, if no further legislation is passed in the meantime, price supports for these basic commodities will revert to prewar levels. The prewar levels, under the Agricultural Adjustment Act of 1938, range between 52 and 75 percent of parity. This same legislation also authorizes loans to producers on any other agricultural commodity at rates to be determined by the Secretary of Agriculture.

2. Section (4) (a) of the Act of July 1, 1941, as amended—the Steagall Amendment—requires price support on not less than 90 percent of parity or comparable price for the non-basic commodities for which the Secretary of Agriculture, by formal public announcement, requested an expanded production for war purposes. The Steagall commodities include hogs; eggs, chickens over 3½ pounds live weight, turkeys, milk and butterfat, dry peas of certain varieties, dry edible beans of certain varieties, soybeans for oil, peanuts for oil, American-Egyptian cotton, potatoes, and sweetpotatoes. The support rates, as in the case of the basic commodities, will be maintained through December 31, 1948.

3. Section (4) (b) of the Act of July 1, 1941, also makes it possible, with certain limitations, to support prices of other commodities. Under this legislation, supports have been provided for wool, cotton linters, naval stores, seeds, sugar beets, sugar cane, and other commodities.

Funds applied to price-support operations during the 1945-46 fiscal year totaled $1,554,000,000. It is estimated that funds applied during the 1946-47 period will total $1,539,000,000.

Sales of commodities acquired under price-support operations may mean a net gain or a net loss, depending upon the circumstances. During the 1945-46 fiscal year, price-support operations were carried on at a net profit of $81,000,000--losses on potatoes, hemp, and wool being more than offset by profits, principally on corn, cotton, tobacco, and wheat. But during the 1946-47 fiscal year, net losses of about $90,000,000 are expected on price-support operations, with losses, mainly on potatoes, hemp, and wool, exceeding profits made on other commodities.

The Corporation inevitably runs the risk of taking losses on its price-support operations. Some commodities, such as grain and cotton, can be stored for years or until such time as it is profitable to dispose of them. But perishable commodities, such as potatoes, chickens, eggs, and the like, must be disposed of in a relatively shorter length of time, regardless of whether the market is favorable or unfavorable.

Existing legislation, in general, prohibits the disposition by the Corporation of farm commodities at less than the parity or comparable price prior to December 31, 1948. There are exceptions. however. Disposals may be made below the parity or comparable price if the commodity has substantially deteriorated in quality or if there is danger of loss or waste through spoilage. Wheat may be sold for feed at not less than the parity price for corn. Commodities may be sold below the parity or comparable price if sold for seed or for new or byproduct uses, or, in the case of peanuts, for the extraction of oil. Surplus potatoes of the 1946 crop may be sold below parity to UNRRA, foreign governments, and the Army--for relief purposes. Any farm commodity may be sold for export at competitive world prices, if such sales will not result in a domestic shortage.

The Supply Program

The Corporation during the war years and up to the present time has acted as "purchasing agent" in the procurement of vast quantities of farm commodities. Under this program--the so-called supply program--the Corporation procures agricultural commodities, foods, and related materials for U. S. Government agencies (principally the Army and Navy), foreign governments, UNRRA, the American Red Cross, and similar organizations. This centralization of operations has meant increased efficiency in procurement and has enabled the Department of Agriculture to coordinate its over-all production and marketing programs.

In the maintenance of food exports to famine areas abroad, the Corporation has played a key part. Total food exports in the 1945-46 fiscal year, for example, reached the unprecedentedly high level of 17,122,000 long tons--and 51 percent of this record tonnage was procured by the Corporation. The previous high record was set in 1919, incidentally, when 14,046,000 long tons were exported.

The Corporation has been especially active in the procurement of grain for relief. During the 1945-46 fiscal year, slightly over 400,000,-000 bushels of grain and grain products in terms of grain equivalent were exported from the United States, a substantial portion of it procured by the Corporation. During the 1946-47 fiscal year, it is expected that exports of U. S. grain will reach 500,000,000 bushels--and again a large part of it will have been procured by the Corporation.

There is a very close relationship,economically, between price-support programs and supply programs. Commodities purchased for price support may be used to meet supply requirements, and purchases for supply needs effectively support domestic prices.

It is the policy of the Corporation to carry on its purchase operations for UNRRA and foreign governments in such a way as to assure the United States against loss. Congress also has taken action to make sure that the Corporation will not suffer losses on supply activities for other Government agencies. Under existing legislation the Corporation must be fully reimbursed for services performed, losses sustained, operating costs incurred, or commodities purchased or delivered to or on behalf of any Government agency, from funds of that agency.

The Corporation tries to "break even" on its supply programs. Net gain during the 1945-46 fiscal year was $338,000. But during the 1946-47 fiscal year, the gain is expected to be substantially larger.

Foreign Purchase Program

The Commodity Credit Corporation is authorized to purchase abroad commodities and products needed for emergency requirements. Such purchases include sugar, fats and oils, rice, and Egyptian cotton. By and large,these purchases implement the allocations made by the International Emergency Food Council.

Purchases of commodities in foreign countries during the 1945-46 fiscal year, exclusive of sugar purchases, amounted to $83,000,000 and during the 1946-47 fiscal year are expected to total about $85,000,000.

Commodity Export Program

Expansion of the export market has long been a prime objective of American agricultural policy. In keeping with that aim, the Commodity Credit Corporation is authorized to export at competitive world prices "any farm commodity or product thereof," provided the commodity or product is not in short supply and provided that the export program will not create a short supply. Because world prices are generally lower than domestic prices, disposals under this authority result in a loss to the Corporation.

Current operations by CCC under this program are limited to cotton acquired in price-support operations. During the 1945-46 fiscal year, operations under the program resulted in a loss of about $32,000,000. Losses during the 1946-47 fiscal year are expected to decline to less than $4,000,000, assuming that the Corporation's established policy will be continued.

Subsidy Programs

During the emergency period, producers' costs were frequently too high to maintain adequate production under price ceilings. To permit the sale of agricultural commodities under the ceilings, and, at the same time, to guarantee producers a fair return, pursuant to direction of the Economic Stabilization Director, the Commodity Credit Corporation, engaged in various subsidy programs.These programs, limited in their scope by Congress, provided for payments on,or purchases of,commodities that were resold at a loss.

The cost of subsidy programs during the 1945-46 fiscal year was $845,000,000. Direct subsidy payments were made on milk and butterfat, beef, fruits, vegetables, sugar, and other commodities. Soybeans were sold at a loss to maintain price ceilings. Wheat and barley were sold at a loss to provide urgently needed livestock feed.

Subsidy operations during the 1946-47 fiscal year are expected to decline to less than $19,000,000. All subsidies, except the one on sugar, have been removed. An increase in the price of sugar, of course, would mean a comparable decrease in the loss incurred by the Corporation.

Loan to the Secretary of Agriculture

The Corporation is required,under terms of the Agricultural Adjustment Act of 1938,to loan to the Secretary of Agriculture sums not in excess of $50,000,000 for Federal crop insurance premium advances, or for advances for soil conservation associations. Repayment of any loan for these purposes is made during the succeeding year from funds appropriated under the Soil Conservation and Domestic Allotment Act.

It can be said without exaggeration that the activities of the Corporation touch every farm family in the United States. The relationship can be direct,as in the case of the farmer who puts his commodities under loan or who sells to a processor required to pay the support price. Or the relationship can be indirect, as when the general price level of a commodity is enhanced by purchases for foreign relief. From an over-all point of view,the Corporation has gone a long way in the direction of its prime objective--the economic stabilization of agricultural production and marketing in the United States.

SURPLUS FOOD DISPOSAL GOES
TO WAR ASSETS ADMINISTRATION

Surplus agricultural commodities and foods will be declared to the War Assets Administration for disposal, instead of to the Department of Agriculture. USDA will offer for disposal property reported to it by owning agencies on or before April 30, 1947. This property is now being inspected and made ready for offering.

Net acquisitions from May 1, 1944, to March 28, 1947, totaled $106,968,702, with a declared cost value of $95,033,882. A total cash return of $8,555,324 was realized from sales, or 93.2 percent of the cost value. Transfers without reimbursement amounted to $2,226,399. Major items sold included coffee, cigarettes, cigars, candy bars, butter, salted peanuts, assorted nuts, vitamin tablets, tea, ice-cream mix, and dried fruit.

Marketing Officials Discuss
Food Distribution Problems

Discussion topics at the annual meeting of the Atlantic States Division of the National Association of Marketing Officials, held in Washington at the U. S. Department of Agriculture April 23-24, included (1) new developments in the fruit and vegetable industry; (2) the Research and Marketing Act of 1946;(3) recent developments relating to market facilities; (4) preservation and identification of quality of foods, from producer to consumer; and (5) proposed amendments to the Agricultural Marketing Agreement Act of 1937.

At the opening session, C. W. Kitchen, executive vice president of the United Fresh Fruit and Vegetable Association, said that the biggest development in food marketing today is the shift from a sellers' to a buyers' market. We will have to sell products, yet we have not learned how to sell all the products we can produce at prices consumers are able and willing to pay. The biggest bottleneck in fresh fruit and vegetable marketing, Kitchen said, is the retail store. His organization is undertaking to help retailers adapt proved methods to their own stores.

As regards the prepackaging of fresh fruits and vegetables, Kitchen said that he personally considers the development as neither a marketing panacea nor a transitory fad. It cannot be a success unless quality is packed and maintained.

Cooperation Needed

He said he did not believe the fruit and vegetable industry alone could solve all the problems concerning the erection of satisfactory market facilities. State and Federal agencies must do much of the necessary research and planning work, and aid in working out and setting up a satisfactory method of financing market facilities over a number of years.

Kitchen commended the results of the USDA's abundant foods program, and said there was room for more promotional work of this kind.

M. W. Baker, assistant director of the PMA Fruit and Vegetable Branch, called for longer range planning to improve fruit and vegetable production, packing, transporting, and merchandising.

F. W. Risher, a NAMO member from Florida, discussed a new dehydration method, being put into operation in his State at Sarasota, for making stock feed from celery tops.

Paul M. Hodgson, member from Delaware, reported on a survey conducted by a Delaware firm of consumer reactions to prepackaged fruits and vegetables, as compared with bulk fresh commodities. According to the study,he said, 72 percent of consumers questioned preferred the prepackaged products to the bulk; 73 percent believed the prepackaged product stayed fresh longer; and 82 percent reported that they left the product in the container while storing it at home until it was ready for use.

E. A. Meyer,administrator of the Research and Marketing Act of 1946 said, that the legislative history of the act clearly had improvement of marketing and marketing services as one of its main purposes. "Research" under the act means simply "investigation" to him, Meyer said--and not necessarily test-tube research.

After pointing out that money is not yet available under the act, and plans thus far are tentative, Meyer discussed these plans and the committee structure now set up.Purpose of the committees is to assemble, process, and coordinate suggestions for specific programs to be carried on under the act. Each commodity advisory committee and functional advisory committee will draw up a priority list of possible projects. From such lists, the 11-man National Advisory Committee will draw up an overall list.

Meyer urged NAMO to work out a means of getting representation for itself with the various commodity and functional groups, which prepare working drafts, embody suggestions for projects, for submission to the commodity and functional advisory committees and through them to the 11-man National Advisory Committee.

Gilmer Speaks

J. B. Gilmer, PMA administrator, pointed out that at present PMA's only connection with the new act is that some PMA personnel are on loan to work up tentative plans for administering the act if funds become available. If and when projects under the act are assigned to PMA, Gilmer said, he expects to arrange PMA organization in such a way as to give them whatever attention they deserve--which,he added, was in his opinion a great deal.

He said that marketing begins even before production;that is, plans for marketing should begin in advance of actual physical production. The organization idea behind PMA is that there is room in one Government bureau for both production and marketing--both in Washington and at different levels in the field. PMA handles work relating to production, marketing, and the Commodity Credit Corporation, and none of these three parts dictates to or is dictated to by any other part. He stated a PMA assistant director for marketing would soon be named.

E. C. Elting, assistant chief of the Office of Experiment Stations, pointed out the need for coordinatiig research affecting the products of various geographical sections of the country.

H. M. Southworth discussed the preference lists of the two commodity committees received thus far by the National Advisory Committee,of which he is executive secretary. In order of priority, the citrus fruit committee listed work on (1) more effective distribution, (2) processing and new uses, (3) quality (standardization as well as market diseases, and (4) in certain production fields. The potato committee listed work on (1) utilization (industrial and food uses) (2) marketing (emphasis on quality improvement and consumer preference), (3) production.

J. H. Meek (Va.) and C.M.White (Maine) discussed the possibilities of developing Federal-State cooperative agreements for carrying on continuous inspection of processed foods, similar to the cooperative agreements now covering inspection of fresh fruits and vegetables.

State-by-State reports, made as the second day of the meeting opened, indicated that many States have submitted suggested projects to the administrator of the Research and Marketing Act, others have worked up a list of such projects but have not yet submitted it, and most of the other States represented are now in position to move rather quickly to submit such lists provided funds are made available. Several speakers pointed out the need for projects dealing with marketing service work, such as market news.

J. S. Larson, of the PMA Marketing Facilities Branch, discussed recent developments in market facilities. These facilities are going to be erected as soon as materials for them are available,he said,--in many cases whether the sponsors have advice from marketing people or not. He offered several precautions to market builders: The lay-out and design should be based on prospective use, and experience in previous markets. The location of facilities should be convenient to all who patronize them. Facilities should not be too large for needs, since space can be added more economically than it can be paid for or subtracted.

In the planning of these facilities, Larson said consideration should be given to frozen foods, the product of a new industry whose sales value in 1945 amounted to over 1 percent of total food sales, and in 1946 was perhaps 50 percent greater.

Surveys Completed

With reference to work being done in the Marketing Facilities Branch, Larson said surveys have been completed on market facilities in 4 cities--Jackson, Miss., New Haven, Conn., and Tampa and Miami, Fla.--and other surveys in 12 other cities are in progress. The surveys ordinarily deal with facilities for fruits, vegetables, poultry, and eggs. Until recently, branch studies of marketing facilities did not go beyond the physical lay-out and buildings. Lately they have begun to include equipment, such as conveyor systems, elevators, lightning, refrigeration rooms, and ripening rooms.

William J. Hackett, NAMO member from Alabama, discussed his State's progress in building markets (12 are completed or under construction). Built and supervised by the State Market Board, they are operated by a farmers' association through an association-named manager. The association obtains title to the property if it pays off the State loan in 20 years. These markets are not being built in areas where private industry is already doing a satisfactory job from the farmers' point of view.

Also under construction in Alabama are six area livestock coliseums.

They will cost $75,000 to $100,000 each, and the State is building them on a matching basis with the counties. Plans are being made to include in them space and equipment for livestock demonstrations--such as demonstrations to housewives of the best methods of cutting meat.

Benjamin P. Storrs (Conn.) discussed work done on market facilities in Connecticut, particularly in Hartford, where progress has reached the point where the legislature has been asked to authorize the State market authority to issue bonds to pay for development. The cost, estimated at 1-1/3 million dollars, would be paid off in 25 years.

Quality Improvement Required

William C. Crow, director of the PMA Marketing Facilities Branch, discussed the preservation and identification of quality foods, from producer to consumer. After naming a number of points in the marketing channel at which quality is reduced, he named four ways of maintaining it: (1) Keeping perishables at proper temperatures all the way from farmer to consumer; (2) eliminating every possible handling operation; (3) speeding up the handling of fresh products; and (4) where quality cannot be maintained if the products are in fresh form, placing them in some form in which it can be maintained.

Besides finding ways of getting quality from the farmer to the consumer, Crow said, we need a way of identifying quality all the way through. That calls for some kind of label. Development of the label form is relatively simple. Development of its use is not so simple. For example, should the top grade, identified by "A", "1", or purpose color--or perhaps all three--be used on the highest 10 percent of production of every commodity, or should it be used on the highest 10 percent of the beef but on the highest 40 percent of the apples? Should the top grade be applied to a certain percentage of each year's output, or always represent a definitely known predetermined quality?

Another problem, Crow said, is deciding which factors should be used to determine the top grade. The consumer will never be ⌐ much interested in buying by grade until he knows (1) that a particular grade suits him better than some other grade, (2) that the product of the grade he selects will always be substantially the same, and (3) that the quality when he gets the product is the same as it was when the grade label was put on the product. This means that grade factors must reflect consumers' preferences, labels must be easily understood, and quality must be preserved from the time the grade label is applied until it is purchased by consumers.

Crow called for enough progress in our methods of grading, labeling, and handling farm food products to label quality properly and understandably and to handle products from the farmer to the consumer with a minimum of deterioration. Then, he said, "Our distributive system will move the right quality to the right market or use, outlets will be expanded, farmers will be remunerated in accordance with the quality they produce, consumers can get what they want and are willing to pay for, and the distributive system will function more efficiently."

Webster J. Birdsall (N.Y.) commented on the need for nutritive value and freshness in food, and the changes in buying habits resulting from the widespread use of home mechanical refrigerators. He stressed the importance of giving the housewife a mark or label "she can get acquainted with," and of Government regulatory work to make sure the quality claimed on the label is in the container.

William C. Crow and S.R. Smith, Director of the PMA Fruit and Vegetable Branch, discussed some of the pending proposed amendments to Agricultural Marketing Agreement Act of 1937. One provides that an administrative agency may collect assessments, to keep its organization in existence, even though the program is currently inoperative. Another provides for bringing under the act commodities not now covered. Another provides that fruit and vegetable marketing agreements need not be suspended when prices rise above parity.

Officers of the Atlantic States Division of NAMO named for the coming year are: W. M. Hackett, (Ala.), chairman, and K. R. Slamp (Pa.), secretary.

NEW TEST FOR PREDICTING BAKING QUALITY OF FLOUR

PMA cereal chemists have found a simple and promising method of testing the baking quality of wheat flour. This is a "sedimentation test" by which a chemist may measure the rate of settling of the solids from an acidified mixture of flour and water and predict the potential bread loaf volume. The test takes only 15 minutes and uses a minimum of laboratory equipment. While this test has been used only for wheat flour, it is expected that further research may show that it could be used successfully in the testing of wheat. The test may be used alone to estimate potential bread loaf volume, or in conjunction with a protein test to determine gluten quality.

The sedimentation test is the result of one of several lines of research being carried on by PMA to devise a test for determining the potential baking quality of wheat. At present, U. S. official grain standards do not adequately reflect the processing value of the wheat. The protein test has been used to indicate the baking quality of wheat but it is not practicable for use at inspection points because it is highly technical and requires expensive and cumbersome equipment. Moreover, it does not indicate the baking quality of flour milled from certain varieties of hard red winter wheat known to have inferior gluten quality.

USDA FOOD DELIVERIES IN MARCH

Deliveries of agricultural commodities and food products by the USDA to foreign governments, UNRRA, and U. S. Government agencies totaled 2,079 million pounds in March. Deliveries to foreign governments totaled 640 million pounds. Of this total, 560 million pounds were grain and grain products; 48 million, potatoes; 18 million, dairy products; 11 million, canned fish; and 3 million, dried eggs. Deliveries to UNRRA amounted to a little under 741 million pounds.

PMA STAFF OFFICERS NAMED

USDA has announced the appointment of two assistant administrators and a deputy assistant administrator for PMA. Dave Davidson, who has been serving as director of the former PMA Field Service Branch, has been appointed Assistant Administrator for Production. His responsibility for production activities will include agricultural conservation and adjustment programs, farm marketing quotas, farm labor supply, and other programs of PMA that involve direct dealings with farmers through the State and county farmer committees. Claudius B. Hodges, Deputy Director of the former Field Service Branch, has been appointed Deputy Assistant Administrator for Production. Carl C. Farrington, Assistant Administrator under the former PMA staff structure, has been appointed Assistant Administrator for Commodity Credit Corporation activities. In his new position, Farrington will be responsible for program finance activities related to loan,price support, foreign supply, domestic diversion and other activities. Appointment of a third PMA assistant administrator--the Assistant Administrator for Marketing--will be announced later. The three assistant administrators will work directly with Administrator Jesse B. Gilmer and Deputy Administrator Ralph S. Trigg in the over-all direction and integration of PMA's programs and services.M.J. Hudtloff has been appointed Comptroller for CCC and PMA. Hudtloff will report directly to the PMA administrator,who is also CCC president,and will have technical authority and responsibility over all fiscal affairs of CCC and PMA,both in Washington and in the field.Since last September Hudtloff has served PMA as deputy assistant administrator for fiscal and inventory control.

SPECIAL ASSISTANT ON WORLD FOOD PROBLEMS APPOINTED

Col. R. L. Harrison,formerly PMA Assistant Administrator in Charge of Fiscal and Inventory Control,has been appointed Special Assistant to the Secretary of Agriculture. In the new post he will undertake any necessary surveys and analyses of the food situation in various areas of the world now partly dependent on food imports from the United States. During the past two years Col. Harrison headed missions that surveyed food conditions in Japan, China, Korea, and most of Europe.

Only five War Food Orders, out of a total of 178 issued, remain in force. These are WFO 7, raw sugar; WFO 10, rice;WFO 144, grain;WFO 63, Food imports; and WFO 78, Enforcement of priority of allocation orders or regulations. Two orders were terminated during April--WFO 51, controlling the production, use, and distribution of edible molasses, and WFO 71, providing procedures by which priorities for the purchase of food were issued and enforced by the U. S. Department of Agriculture. An additional order, WFO 2, butter,requiring manufacturers to set aside certain percentages of their production for sale to Government agencies, was terminated in May.

Rice--Production and Marketing

....By Grace E. M. Waite

If you are an average rice eater, your consumption of rice this year will be somewhere in the neighborhood of 5 pounds. But you probably aren't average. If you live in one of the Southeastern States, for example, your consumption of this food may reach 50 pounds. Or, should you be a New Englander, chances are you will use barely 2 pounds.

Per capita consumption of milled rice has varied considerably from the 1935-39 prewar average of 5.6 pounds. Consumption in 1943 was 5.8 pounds; in 1944, 4.9; in 1945, 4.8; and in 1946, 4.2. This decline in consumption is directly traceable to the substantial quantities of rice required for war purposes and for postwar relief feeding.

Big Crop

The fact that the per capita supply estimated as available to domestic consumers, 5.0 pounds, is slightly larger this year than last does not mean that food needs abroad have slackened materially. It is, rather, a reflection of a big United States crop. The 1946 rice crop set a new high record--71,520,000 bushels, as compared with 68,150,000 bushels in 1945, and a 10-year (1935-44) average of 55,257,000 bushels. But we are sharing this big crop, under international allocation, with U. S. armed forces, U.S. Territories, Cuba, the Philippines, UNRRA, and other claimants. A set-aside order under WFO 10 implemented these allocations until April 1, 1947, when the set-aside was reduced to zero. Rice is still scarce and is one of the few products remaining under a ceiling price.

You can be sure that the rice supply this year will be larger than it was in the days before the Revolutionary War when the industry was getting started. These early attempts to establish rice production in the United States are described in "Rice Production and Marketing in the United States"--USDA Miscellaneous Publication 615--by George A. Collier, of PMA's Grain Branch. In this interesting and timely publication, Mr. Collier goes on to discuss modern production methods, marketing practices, and Government services available to the rice industry.

According to Collier, rice growing in the United States got its first real start in South Carolina about 1685. Later, production expanded into North Carolina, Georgia, and Florida.

The Civil War adversely affected production in the South Atlantic States. So rice growing began to shift westward. Today, rice production is concentrated in four States--Louisiana, Texas, California, and Arkansas (in that order of importance).

Collier says rice in the United States is grown about the same way as other grain crops, such as wheat, oats, and barley. The big difference is the factor of irrigation; the land is kept 4 to 8 inches under heads are nearly ripe and the crop is ready for harvest. About the same kinds of machinery are used to harvest rice as are used for other cereal grains.

In the South, rice is seeded usually with a grain drill or a broadcast seeder,but most California rice growers flood their fields and take to the air to do their seeding. An airplane equipped with a hopper near the pilot's seat carries around 600 pounds of seed—enough to sow 5 or 6 acres. As the seed runs out of the hopper, the draft from the propeller scatters it evenly over a strip 30 to 50 feet wide. A flagman on the ground helps to guide the pilot. Seeding rice into water allows the seed to germinate and take root. It also prevents birds from eating the seed. Weeds are eliminated because their seeds will not root in water.

When rice is harvested the kernels ordinarily contain 20 to 30 percent of moisture. This is too much because, for good milling quality and safe storage, rice should contain not more than 14 percent of moisture. Consequently, the rice must be dried—in a home-made drier or a commercial rice drier.

Three general types of rice are grown in the United States—short-, medium-, and long-grain rice. Short-grain varieties are grown principally in California, medium- and long-grain varieties principally in the South.

The rice the farmer grows is commonly called rough rice after it is threshed.The grain has a rough hull and looks a little like oats or barley. The rough rice, after the farmer disposes of it, must be milled before it is suitable for table use.

Rice milling is just the opposite of wheat milling. In wheat milling,the object is to break down the kernels into flour,but in rice milling the object is to keep the kernels intact. After the rice is cleaned, to remove chaff, weed seeds, and foreign material the milling process begins. The hulls are removed from the kernels and the resulting brown rice is further processed to remove the brown bran coat. The rice is scoured and polished. It is then graded or sized, to separate the small broken pieces from the whole kernels and larger pieces. Millers sometimes give rice a high polish with a final coating of glucose and talc.

Rice Marketing

Most rough rice goes to the mill, but some is used on the farm for food, feed, and seed. Growers sell most of their crop direct to millers or their buyers, since most of the mills are in, or close to,the producing area. A limited quantity of rough rice is sold for feed or to dealers for export. However, growers may store their rice in elevators or warehouses until it is sold.

Millers sell their processed rice to jobbers, wholesalers, or chain store systems. Some millers have sales agencies and storage warehouses in the large markets, and others handle their transactions through brokers. Jobbers and wholesalers sell to retail stores.

Prior to World War II a little more than half the rice we produced was used in this country. The rest was shipped to Puerto Rico, the Virgin Islands, Hawaii, Alaska, or other countries. On the basis of first quarter allocations for 1947, somewhat less than half of the 1946 production will be available to U. S. civilians.

U. S. Standards

U. S. standards established for rough and milled rice, covering quality and condition, enable growers and members of the industry to market their grain to the best advantage. The 11 rough rice classes cover the principal commercial varieties. There are 6 numerical grades in each class and a sample grade for rice that does not meet the requirements of the numerical grades. The percentages of damaged kernels, red rice, cereal grains, and rice of other classes largely determine the grade. Special grades cover damp, seedy, muddy, chalky, weevily, and musty rough rice.

Milled and brown rice are divided into nine classes, which correspond to classes I-IX for rough rice. The wholesale trade buys largely on the basis of these standards. Each class of milled rice includes seven official grades—six of them numerical grades and the other a sample grade. There are four U. S. official grades for each of the two classes of brown rice—California brown rice and southern brown rice.

Federal or Federal-State inspection offices are located in all the principal production areas. At these offices, licensed inspectors for a small fee will analyze and determine the class and grade of rough rice, and issue a certificate on the milling quality which indicates the percentages of whole milled rice, broken kernels, and moisture.

Weevil infestation and odor, both grade factors, are determined when the sample is drawn. Grade tests are made in the laboratory for the milling quality and the moisture content of rough rice. "Milling quality" means the resistance to breakage of rice in milling, or the quantity of whole-grain rice and broken rice that is obtained from a unit of rough rice. The most important factors besides moisture content in determining the grade of milled rice are general appearance, number of weed seeds present, and proportion of broken and damaged kernels.

Before July 1946 the ceiling on southern rice was based on a 17 percent moisture content, an increasing discount being allowed as the moisture content increased above 17 percent. Farmers received a premium for rice containing not more than the prescribed amount of moisture.

When the 1946 crop was marketed, a premium was authorized for rice that was drier than was formerly specified. To provide additional facilities for rice inspection, the Federal-State inspection service expanded its operations to supply official certification to producers. To December 31, 1946, more than 11 million barrels of rough rice were inspected under the expanded service. Rice containing 14 percent moisture (or less) qualified for a premium payment of 60 cents a barrel. Smaller premiums were paid on rice containing between 14 and 17 percent of moisture.

MARKETING BRIEFS:

Meat and Livestock.—Revised hog support prices for the final six months of the 1946-47 marketing year—the April-September 1947 period—will average $1.35 per hundred pounds higher than the schedule announced last October. Weekly prices, which will continue seasonal variations are based on an annual average support price of $15.60 per hundred pounds, Chicago basis, as compared with the average of $14.25 in effect from October 1946 through March 1947. The revision results from the recent sharp increase in parity. It is also in accordance with the recently approved policy that the hog support price be established at 90 percent of parity—as required by law—at the beginning of the two marketing seasons, spring and fall, during the marketing year.... Livestock shippers' proceeds, from sales of livestock, that have been deposited in a separate account designated as a "Custodial Account for Shippers' Proceeds" by commission firms will be insured up to $5000 for each consignor having an interest in the account, under an arrangement with the Federal Deposit Insurance Corporation. Previously, when a commission firm deposited shippers' proceeds in a separate account in an insured bank, the entire amount deposited, regardless of the sum, was insured only up to $5000 and for the benefit of the commission firm only. Commission firms operating at several stockyards posted under the Packers and Stockyards Act have already established the required custodial accounts. Action has been started to amend regulations issued under the Packers and Stockyards Act to provide for the establishment and maintenance by all registered commission firms of separate custodial accounts for handling proceeds of sales of shippers' livestock.... No "cures" will be used in the Mexican-United States campaign to suppress the outbreak of foot-and-mouth disease in Mexico because none has been found to be effective. Foot-and-mouth disease is caused by a highly infective virus and is one of the most devastating animal diseases known. The time lost by the use of these "cures" would result in further spread of the virus, hinder eradication work and make it more expensive. Plans call for drastic quarantine and slaughter of affected and exposed animals, followed by thorough cleaning and disinfection of premises.

Fruits and Vegetables.—An amendment to the marketing agreement and order regulating the handling of California Bartlett pears, plums, and Elberta peaches, during the current marketing season has been put into effect to regulate the shipment of plums into, in, or through (1) the San Francisco-Sacramento region, consisting of Marin County, Sacramento County, Contra Costa County, Alameda County, San Mateo County, and San Francisco County; and (2) the Los Angeles region, consisting of Ventura County, Los Angeles County, and Orange County.. An amendment to ICC Service Order 180 to extend through May 31, with respect to demurrage on refrigerator cars, provides that the first two days shall be free, third day $2.20, fourth day $5.50, and each day thereafter $11. Unless extended after May 31, rates will revert to those in effect since July 1, 1946—first two days free, third and fourth days each $2.20, fifth day $5.50, sixth day $11, seventh day $22, and each succeeding day $44....Florida citrus industry is pushing a State "master brand" which could be used by any shipper whose fruit met specified quality standards....Nearly 11 million bushels of potatoes from the 1946 crop have been shipped abroad under the USDA's potato export program, providing needed food supplies for deficit areas abroad and an outlet for approximately 10 percent of last year's potato surplus....Being placed in operation is a marketing order regulating the handling of Irish potatoes grown in Michigan, Wisconsin, Minnesota, and North Dakota during 1947. Potato industry representatives of this area have recommended operation of the program to keep low quality potatoes off the commercial market and give consumers better quality potatoes.

Sugar and Molasses.--Price control of sugar, transferred to USDA along with sugar rationing by Congressional act on March 31,is expected by the Sugar Rationing Administration to be made more effective and uniform by revival of the community pricing program on May 1. All the regulations and forms in effect on the date of the transfer, March 31, remain effective unless changed by USDA....Sugar allotments about 25 percent larger have been announced for restaurants, hotels, hospitals, and other institutional users by USDA's Sugar Rationing Administration for the May-June period..War Food Order 51,which controlled production, use, and distribution of edible molasses, was terminated April 21,1947.

Fats and Oils.--Fats and oils export allocations for the second quarter of 1947 totaled 92,700,000 pounds as of May 12. This amount includes 5,600,000 pounds allocated to export claimants in exchange for other fats and oils needed in the United States....Oleomargarine production for the first quarter of 1947 totaled 204 million pounds, compared to 140 million for the first quarter of 1946. About 5-1/2 million pounds were exported during January-March 1947. First quarter production at an annual rate of 834 million pounds compares with 573 million in 1946,and 614 million pounds (all-time high) in 1945....The farm price of 1947-crop farmers stock peanuts will be supported at 90 percent of parity as of July 15, 1947, the beginning of the marketing year. Prices will be supported by CCC loans and purchases. Purchase and loan values by type, sound mature kernel content, and quality, based on historical differences in value, will be announced after the July parity price has been determined.

Poultry.--A price-support program has been announced for 1947-crop turkeys marketed from October 1, 1947, through January 31, 1948. USDA will buy dressed turkeys from processors who certify that they have paid producers not less than the liveweight support prices to be announced about October 1. These prices will reflect a national average price of not less than 90 percent of the September 15 parity price for turkeys. Support prices and the purchase prices to be announced for dressed turkeys will vary according to the four production zones in which a program is now in effect in support of producer prices for breeding stock. The price-support program for breeder stock ends June 30, 1947. No support program will be set up for breeder hens or toms in 1948.

Eggs.--Egg prices will be supported in the Midwest in June through the purchase of dried and frozen eggs at the May level, which reflects an average price to producers of 35 cents a dozen for shell eggs. This will protect producers in areas of surplus production.

Dairy.--There is some indication of a post-war shift back to farm-separated cream and increased use of skim milk for livestock feed rather than for powder manufacture. To check the accuracy of reports on such a shift, PMA is preparing a questionnaire directed to the Government's 27 milk powder plants to see whether there has been a noticeable decrease in amounts of skim milk received...Tentative approval has been announced of an amendment to Federal Order 42,which regulates milk handling in the New Orleans, La., milk market to revise the basis formula price and class price differentials, and establish a plan of seasonal price adjustment. Producer approval or disapproval of the proposed amendment will be determined at the same time the new marketing agreement is submitted to handlers for signature.

Grain.--An estimated 1,500,000 long tons (58,133,000 bushels) of United States grain and grain products were exported in April, raising the total for the 10 months, July through April to 10,973,000 long tons (426,583,000 bushels, of which 315,093,000 bushels were wheat and flour equivalent). About 65 percent of the 10 months total were exported by PMA and the remainder through commercial trade channels.

Cotton.--U. S. Commercial Company (RFC subsidiary) has announced a program to permit private buyers to bring Japanese cotton gray goods into U. S. for finishing here and re-export. To ensure reshipment abroad, a surety bond of 10 cents per linear yard must be posted with USCC. Offers to purchase must be for at least 1 million yards and must be accompanied by a certified check for either 5 or 20 percent of the purchase price, depending on the terms of sale. Limited quantities of print cloths, sheetings, jeans, and drills made in Japan are now available under this program. Persons· interested in buying these goods should apply to USCC at New York or Washington or to any of the RFC loan agencies in principal cities....The cotton export subsidy has been reduced from 2 cents per pound to 1/2 cent per pound, gross unpatched weight, effective May 8, 1947....Total carryover of cotton in U. S. on August 1 is expected to be about 3 million bales--60 percent smaller than last year's carryover, and smallest since 1929.

ADVISORY COMMITTEE MEETINGS

Meetings of advisory committees to develop programs under the Research and Marketing Act have been held and policies formed for the following: Cotton, potatoes, citrus, poultry, cottonseed (sub-committee of cotton), peanuts, deciduous fruits, and transportation.

Scheduled meetings of committees for the following commodities are: Beans and peas, June 2-3; seeds, June 4-5; vegetables, June 5-6; tree nuts, June 9-10; wool, June 10-11; rice,June 11-12;dairy products, June 12-13; grain, June 16-17; soybeans-flaxseed June 17-18;livestock, June 19-20; feeds, June 23-24; fisheries, June 24-25; sugar,June 25-26; and tobacco, June 26-27. A meeting of the National Advisory Committee will start June 30.

ABOUT MARKETING

The following addresses and publications, issued recently, may be obtained upon request. To order, check on this page the publications desired, detach and mail to the Production and Marketing Administration, U. S. Department of Agriculture, Washington 25, D. C.

Addresses and Statements:

Long-Range Agricultural Policy, by Clinton P. Anderson, Secretary of Agriculture, at hearings of House Committee on Agriculture, April 21, 1947. 19 pp. (Mimeographed)

Cooperation is Keynote of the Americas, by Clinton P. Anderson,Secretary of Agriculture, Washington, D. C. April 16, 1947. 4 pp. (Mimeographed)

A Challenge for Agriculture, by Jesse B. Gilmer, Administrator of PMA and President of CCC, Dallas, Texas. April 12, 1947. 8 pp. (Mimeographed)

Research in Marketing Agricultural Products, by E.A. Meyer, Administrator, Research and Marketing Act of 1946, Seattle,Wash. May 2, 1947. 12 pp. (Mimeographed)

What's Ahead in Cotton? by C. C. Smith, Assistant Director, Cotton Branch, PMA, Augusta, Ga. May 3, 1947. 6 pp. (Mimeographed)

Identification and Preservation of Quality of Foods from Producers to Consumers, by William C. Crow, Director, Marketing Facilities Branch, Washington, D. C. April 23, 1947. 4 pp. (Mimeographed)

Recent Developments in Marketing Facilities, by J. Stanford Larson. Marketing Facilities Branch, Washington, D. C. April 23, 1947. 6 pp. (Mimeographed)

Publications:

The Wholesale Fruit and Vegetable Markets of Tampa, Fla. (PMA in cooperation with the Florida Agricultural Experiment Station, Florida Agricultural Extension Service, and Florida State Department of Agriculture) April 1947. 70 pp. (Mimeographed)

Relation and Relative Importance of Some Cotton Fiber Properties to Certain Manufacturing Qualities. (PMA) February 1947. 22 pp. (Multilithed)

Effect of Cleaning on Grade and Color of Cotton. (PMA) April 1947. 26 pp. (Multilithed)

Price-Support Programs for Gum Naval Stores, 1934-46. (PMA) March 1947. 34 pp. (Mimeographed)

1947 Loan and Price-Support Programs. (PMA) April 1947. 8 pp. (Mimeographed)

The Commodity Credit Corporation. (PMA) April 1947. 7 pp. (Mimeographed)

State Agricultural Departments and Marketing Agencies, with Names of Officials. (PMA) Revised April 1947. 7 pp. (Mimeographed)

U.S. Standards for Berries for Processing. Effective June 2, 1947. 3 pp. (Mimeographed)

Rules of Practice Under the Commodity Exchange Act. (Commodity Exchange Authority) May 1947. 49 pp. (Mimeographed)

Dairying in War and Peace. F. M. 61 (Bureau of Agricultural Economics) March 1947. 61 pp. (Multilithed)

Field and Seed Crops, Acreage, Yield and Production. Revised Estimates, 1939-44, by States. (Bureau of Agricultural E conomics) April 1947. 56 pp. (Multilithed)

Outline of a Sanitation Program for the Poultry Industry. (Bureau of Animal Industry) April 1947. 10 pp. (Multilithed)

CPSIA information can be obtained
at www.ICGtesting.com
Printed in the USA
BVHW041351280119
538843BV00005B/366/P

9 780331 398144